, and you set a good
ure. **Enliv**   r.
sponsibility. Educat
 live. Instruction do
nent everything. See
now yourself: **now t**
everence, educate
 them forth in **free**
 teacher, but they a

vill today, and you se

or the future. **Enlive**

h, **feel** responsibility

ourage to live. Instr

couragement everyt

child, know yourse

ildren in **reverenc**

and send them fort

being is a teacher

THE
WISDOM
OF
Waldorf

The Wisdom of Waldorf has been handcrafted by the people of Floris Books, contributions joyfully sought, carefully edited and lovingly designed by a team dedicated to sharing knowledge and wisdom with the world. This book was printed on sustainable paper. We hope it will be a positive contribution to our world.

First published in 2019 by Floris Books
Compilation © 2019 Floris Books
The Sources section forms part of the copyright of this book

British Library CIP Data available
978-178250-611-9

Printed in Poland through Hussar

 Floris Books supports sustainable forest management by
printing this book on materials made from wood that comes
from responsible sources and reclaimed material

THE
WISDOM
OF
Waldorf

100 Reflections
on Waldorf Education to
Enrich and Inspire

Floris
Books

~

Introduction

~

The celebration of one hundred years of Waldorf education lifts the hearts of countless individuals in dozens of countries that reach around this globe of ours – from China to Africa, Canada to Australia, and Russia to Brazil. Teachers, educators, parents and former Waldorf students come together in this book to reflect on their own experiences and the lessons Waldorf education has taught all of us over the past century.

It is almost impossible to experience Waldorf education in any way and *not* be changed by it – inspired, redirected, pushed to think. When it was introduced by Rudolf Steiner and Emil Molt in 1919, it was a response by these two visionary friends to the misery of World War I. It arose from a belief that human beings can be lifted out of deepest despair through sharing and learning. The Waldorf approach is based on:

- **love**,
- **artistic digestion** towards the wisdom underlying all knowledge,

- **rigour** that comes from strong willpower cultivated within each individual, and on
- **trust** that once young people have an experience, they will draw conclusions of their own and then go on to discover what others before them have articulated about the matter.

In this unique collection, Floris Books has assembled thoughts from those who, over a hundred years, have imagined Waldorf education into existence, and who have been changed by their involvement, alongside some of Rudolf Steiner's most inspirational thoughts on teaching and education. These enriching quotes provide a reflection of the changes that have occurred around the world in the hearts of those who have discovered Waldorf education, experienced it and now describe it. The thoughts and ideas assembled here define this new imagination, the fresh picture – of how Waldorf education has opened up the space in which lasting and authentic change can occur.

Patrice Maynard
Director of Publications and Development at the Research Institute for Waldorf Education, USA

Preface

Back in the 1970s, when I first came across Steiner-Waldorf education, I would have benefitted from a book like this one. As a conventionally trained teacher who set up what was then called a 'remedial unit' in the Middle School where I taught, I became disillusioned by the poor treatment of and lack of care for the children who were sent to me. I started looking for alternative, more humane and integrated types of education.

An article about a Steiner school for children with additional needs fell into my hands. Wanting to find out more, the local library of a small Norfolk market town was my starting point: 'Yes, we do have a book by Dr Rudolf Steener [sic]… It's called *Occult Science*.' (The librarian sounded dubious.) Several renewals later, I had managed to read less than half of that book, understanding less than half of that. And I still hadn't worked out what the book had to do with education.

I persisted, in part, because I was intrigued and partly because I was not sure whether the author was mad. If mad, however, it seemed to me a very sober, carefully considered madness. By then, having visited some Waldorf schools and read more about the education, it dawned on me that there was an unconventional but vital wisdom in all this. I came to recognise Steiner as one of the first great truly inclusive thinkers. The richness of imagination I observed in Waldorf practice lead me to find a vocation in Steiner-Waldorf schools for, at their best, they placed humanity and the potential of young people at their heart.

A book of quotations, such as this, cannot present a full map of Waldorf education. What it does offer is a selection of key points for orientation, or a profusion of thought-buds. In a world in which the schools, in common with humanity as a whole, face great challenges, the inspiration that can be gained from the words contained here is for everyone who brings an open mind, heart and intention to them.

Kevin Avison
Executive officer and senior adviser,
Steiner Waldorf Schools Fellowship, UK

100 Reflections

We do not **teach** children merely for the years during which they are under our care, but to benefit their **whole** lives.

Rudolf Steiner

"If the nursery class nourishes the soul of the child by providing a spiritual experience of the rhythms of the season, it is also feeding a starving world."

A.C. Harwood
author and co-founder of Michael Hall school, UK

" **Little** thoughts will get us nowhere, so we must pluck up the courage to think **big** thoughts. "

Rudolf Steiner

"The object of Steiner-Waldorf education is to aid children so that as adults they may bring their powers, their own **innate** sacred human qualities, to greater **fulfilment**."

Francis Edmunds
founder of Emerson College, UK

"We must always take care
that, as teachers, we create
what goes from us to the
children in an **exciting**
way so that it gives rise to
imagination.

Rudolf Steiner

"
Preparing the soil is the gardeners' duty
and they marvel as plants of different kinds
reveal in shape and colour their **beauty**.
Likewise, we see how our children grow,
each on their way to their personal **bloom**,
their talents and chances more than we know.
"

Willem van der Velden
academic head of the Centre for
Curative Education, South Africa

"Teachers say to themselves that here is a human being from whom relationships extend out to the entire **cosmos**, and when I do my work with every one of these **growing** children, I do something that has **meaning** for the entire cosmos."

Rudolf Steiner

"Children **learn** more from being **bored** than from being **entertained**."

Douglas Gerwin
executive director of the Research Institute
for Waldorf Education, USA

"**Learning** is a contextual reality… If there is something you wish your students to learn, you must **live** it."

Jon McAlice
co-founder of the Center for
Contextual Studies, USA

"Every human being is a teacher, but they are sleeping and must be **awakened**, and **art** is the awakener…"

Rudolf Steiner

It is easy to forget the fundamental **significance** of education, which is to educate the whole human being – for **life**.

Eric G. Müller

educator and founder of the
Alkion Teacher Training Programme, USA

"Through loving care, **joy-filled** teaching and our own **self-development,** we educators provide the conditions for children to develop into self-determining human beings."

Janni Nicol
early childhood executive officer at the
Steiner Waldorf Schools Fellowship, UK

For every one step
you take in the pursuit
of higher knowledge,
take three steps in
the perfection of your
own **character.**

Rudolf Steiner

The **belief, love** and **hope** of all human beings connect themselves to children wherever they appear.

Helmut von Kügelgen
founder of the International Association
of Waldorf Kindergartens

"Children do not learn through instruction or admonition, but through **imitation**.

Rudolf Steiner

"Waldorf education has the *potential* to greatly benefit children of all countries, all ethnicities, all socio-economic groups and all religions and none."

Neil Boland
lecturer at Auckland University
of Technology, New Zealand

"As soon as you approach children with **love**, your educating becomes effective.

Rudolf Steiner

A good **toy** is 90% child and 10% toy.

Joan Almon
former educator and co-general secretary
of the Anthroposophical Society, USA

> Receive the children
> in **reverence**,
> educate them in **love**,
> and send them forth
> in **freedom**.

Rudolf Steiner

"The developing child has the dual task of **uniting** their spiritual soul with their temporal body, as well as **emancipating** themselves from its constrictions and traditions. The teacher's task is to **support** the child in both endeavours."

Sven Saar
educator and advisor to the
Steiner Waldorf Schools Fellowship, UK

"We are fully human only while **playing**, and we play only when we are **human** in the truest sense of the word."

Friedrich Schiller

"Children possess the whole **creative** faith and do not yet have the seed of destructive reason. They are innocent and, therefore, wise."

Federico García Lorca
poet and playwright

"Human beings must be capable of **feeling**, not weakly, but strongly: beautiful – ugly, good – evil, true – false, so that they live in them with their whole **being**.

Rudolf Steiner

What we need to practise more than anything else in today's world is **self-discipline.** The pupils of the Waldorf School should be able to stand as an **example** for others in this.

Emil Molt
co-founder of the first Waldorf school

"We must realise that our work with young people is a **continuation** of what higher beings have done before birth."

Rudolf Steiner

"There is never a bad child, only unfulfilled needs."

Henning Köhler
author and educator

"My Steiner education has ensured that I approach my work with **sincerity**, **perspective** and, **most** importantly, **play**.

Daniel Beasley

architect

"**Truth** is a seed present in every human being. If we devote ourselves to the development of that essence, the seed can **blossom**."

Rudolf Steiner

"Without **imagination** we cannot foresee, organise or originate what is needed for the **future**."

Christy MacKaye Barnes
author, educator, speech artist and poet

"A human being can experience **freedom** only when the intellect can awaken on its own from **within**.

Rudolf Steiner

"When the Waldorf curriculum is carried out successfully, the whole human being – head, heart and hands – has been truly educated.

Henry Barnes
educator and founder of
Hawthorne Valley Waldorf School, USA

"The whole point of
a **kindergarten** is to
give young children
the opportunity to
imitate life in a simple
and wholesome way."

Rudolf Steiner

Instruction does much, but **encouragement** everything.

Johann Wolfgang von Goethe
writer and philosopher

"We dare not have **enthusiasm** merely for our special tasks. We can only be good teachers when we have a living interest in **everything** happening in the world."

Rudolf Steiner

"When I went to the Steiner school for the first time, I was struck mainly by older children: I had never before walked into a school where teenagers were so **welcoming** and self-possessed and **kind**."

Tilda Swinton

actor

Children must be taught **how** to think, not **what** to think.

Margaret Mead

anthropologist

We must be educated in inner human **modesty**, so we can recognise that we are not, even for a moment, complete as human beings. Instead, we continue to **develop** from birth until death.

Rudolf Steiner

"To be able to see the world as someone else sees it, to treat your neighbour as yourself, requires a very special quality: **imagination.**"

Andrew Hill
head teacher at Glenaeon
Rudolf Steiner School, Australia

Essentially, there is no education other than **self-education**. We have to provide the conditions where children can educate themselves according to their own **destinies**.

Rudolf Steiner

"Waldorf education is the consistent answer to the **challenges** of our time."

Richard Landl
president of the European Council for
Steiner Waldorf Education

"Even the **wisest** can **learn** incalculably much from children."

Rudolf Steiner

Don't demand anything from the children, but demand it from **yourself** and see if the children come along with you.

Willi Müller
founder of the Eugene Teacher
Education Programme, USA

Every child should stand before the soul of the teacher as a **question** posed.

Rudolf Steiner

"When I am asked, "What did Waldorf education do for you?" I reply, "It **encouraged** me to always **strive** to become a better human being."

Jens Stoltenberg
thirteenth Secretary General of NATO and former
Prime Minister of Norway

The golden rule of education is to go from movement to **rest**, from the active to the **passive**, from will to **intellect**.

A.C. Harwood
author and co-founder of Michael Hall school, UK

"Our work to support healthy child development is only sustainable if we **collaborate** not only with our human colleagues, but also with the **spiritual** forces that are waiting for us to call on them."

Jill Tina Taplin

course co-ordinator at the North of England Steiner Waldorf
Early Childhood Studies Programme, UK

Where is the **book** in which the teacher can read about what teaching is? The children **themselves** are the book.

Rudolf Steiner

"Education is the great engine of personal development.
It is through **education** that the daughter of a peasant can become a doctor, that the son of a mineworker can become the head of the mine, that a child of farmworkers can **become** the president of a great nation.

Nelson Mandela

"We must not receive this art of education as a theory, we must not take it as something we can learn. We should receive it as something with which we can **unite** ourselves."

Rudolf Steiner

"Fairy tales do not tell children that dragons exist. Children already know that dragons exist. Fairy tales tell children that dragons can be beaten."

G.K. Chesterton
author, and literary and art critic
(revised by Neil Gaiman)

> We need to learn that each new day and each new year offers continual **revelation**.

Rudolf Steiner

"We do not inherit the **earth** from our ancestors. We **borrow** it from our children."

Chief Seattle
Suquamish and Duwamish chief

"Just as everything is growing and **changing** all the time, so whatever teachers give to their pupils should also **grow** and change; it should remain **alive**."

Rudolf Steiner

A general liveliness and cheerfulness prevails, combined with golden humour. This is the atmosphere in which Waldorf School children grow up.

Berta Molt
co-founder of the first Waldorf school

"It is not our task to convey convictions to the next generation. They must use their own judgement, their own **perception**. They should learn to **look** into the world with open eyes."

Rudolf Steiner

I am deeply **grateful** for Waldorf education, which woke me up and helped me **rediscover** my imagination.

Michael Ende
author

"Educating is providing **courage** to live."

Henning Köhler
educator and author

> It seems natural that doing comes first, and thinking follows after.

Emil Molt
co-founder of the first Waldorf school

"There should be a Waldorf school for **adults,** for all of us who wish we had a Waldorf education and did not.

Ronald E. Koetzsch

editor of *Renewal: A Journal for Waldorf Education*

"Reverence, enthusiasm, and a sense of guardianship; these three are actually the panacea, the magical remedy, in the soul of the educator.

Rudolf Steiner

"Waldorf **education** doesn't exist. What exists are 40,000 Waldorf **teachers** worldwide."

Wolfgang Held
author and Communications director
at the Goetheanum, Switzerland

An **imaginative** teacher will make the most stony ground **grow** charming flowers of **fantasy.**

A.C. Harwood
author and co-founder of Michael Hall school, UK

"As soon as you **approach** a child with **love**, your educating becomes effective, becomes a powerful thing."

Rudolf Steiner

"What has the most profound impact on students' learning is their teacher's daily striving to be a better and more rounded human being.

Warren Cohen

educator and former director of the
Rudolf Steiner Centre, Canada

"Values cannot be separated from education any more than air can be cleansed of oxygen. Education without **values** is no longer education.

Douglas Gerwin
executive director of the Research Institute
for Waldorf Education, USA

Life flows **freely,** unhindered, back and forth from teacher to pupil.

Rudolf Steiner

" I never teach my pupils,
I only attempt to
provide the **conditions**
in which they can **learn**. "

Albert Einstein

"What is learned by heart must first be understood.

Rudolf Steiner

"By embracing the child with loving **interest** we find out what the child needs. This opens our hearts to the child's greater inherent **potential**."

Wolfgang Maschek
tutor at Melbourne Rudolf Steiner Seminar, Australia

You will only
move forward
if you think
in a **circle**.

Rudolf Steiner

"Waldorf education builds young people able to think **clearly** and independently, to consider all aspects of life before deciding to be **ethical** and compassionate. It's only this kind of education that will change the world."

Patrice Maynard

director of Publications and Development at the
Research Institute for Waldorf Education, USA

"Thinking engendered through Waldorf schooling – mobile, fluid thinking – is in tune with life, for it is in itself, **alive.**"

David Mitchell

educator and co-founder of Waldorf Publications

"What's so **wonderful** about Waldorf education is you're exposed to all these different ideas, but you're never given one view of it. You're encouraged to think as an **individual**."

Julianna Margulies
actor

"The **heart** of the Waldorf method is that education is an art – it must speak to children's **experience**.

Rudolf Steiner

If I was to sum up what Steiner-Waldorf education gave me, it was attitude. The **courage** to dream big and follow those dreams with **passion** and **integrity**.

Yanto Barker
former professional cyclist

It is education which serves the **freedom** of the human spirit.

Francis Edmunds
founder of Emerson College, UK

"The less we try to explain to children, the more they can make of the world."

Jon McAlice
co-founder of the Center for
Contextual Studies, USA

"The real educational value of **play** lives in the fact that we ignore our rules and regulations, our educational theory, and allow children **free** rein."

Rudolf Steiner

"The end result of Waldorf education is to raise our consciousness. It taught me to think for myself, to be **responsible** for my decisions. It made me **sensitive** to the needs of others, and it helped establish **meaningful** beliefs."

Kenneth Chenault
former chair and CEO of American Express

"Teachers must be the representative of the true, the good, and the beautiful. Children must be drawn to **truth**, **goodness**, and **beauty** simply because they are drawn to their teacher."

Rudolf Steiner

"Both the simplest childlike **feelings** and the wisest forms of **knowledge** come together in fairy tales."

Rudolf Meyer

author

"Enter the classroom in such a way that your **words** carry **weight** and, at the same time, acquire **wings.**"

Rudolf Steiner

"It was my experience at a Waldorf school that encouraged me to pursue acting as a career. It was a **free-spirited** school that encouraged **creativity** and individualism."

Jennifer Aniston

actor

If one **guides** children in such a way that they can develop **gratitude** for even the most unimportant or trivial things, then those children will not egotistically close themselves off from the world.

Rudolf Steiner

"What we do not understand, we do not possess.

Johann Wolfgang von Goethe
writer and philosopher

"Much of what Steiner said about child development in 1919 now looks **remarkably** prescient."

John Davy
chair of the Anthroposophical Society of Great Britain
and science correspondent for *The Observer*

"In the material word, we effect change through what we **do**; as educators, we effect change through who we **are**.

Rudolf Steiner

"Playing outside should be a subject at school."

Johan Cruyff
professional football player and coach

"I wanted to **open** the **door** to education for all children, regardless of their parents' income."

Emil Molt
co-founder of the first Waldorf school

> I cannot teach anybody anything, I can only make them **think.**

Socrates

"Creative ability **opens** the door to practical life."

John F. Gardner
author and educator

"Every assembly, every performance, whether eurythmy, gymnastics or music, brings a **transformation** of mood. The shadows recede, the **light** breaks through."

Emil Molt
co-founder of the first Waldorf school

"Rudolf Steiner wrote that **ideals** are to a child's soul what the skeleton is to the body – nothing less than the **scaffolding** that young people need for stability, strength and direction."

David Sloan

author, lecturer and founding teacher of
Merriconeag Waldorf School, USA

For young children, **play** creates the opportunity to digest past experiences and thus come to **understand** them.

Loïs Eijgenraam
author, educational consultant and lecturer

What the teacher imparts of their own **experience** is a pillar of **strength** for the child wishing to penetrate through the darkness to **light.**

Rudolf Steiner

"Like intelligence, our feelings need schooling to become rich and mature. Then they can guide us from within as an inner understanding."

Andrew Hill
head teacher at Glenaeon
Rudolf Steiner School, Australia

"It is a **blessing** if, in later years, one can look back with deep satisfaction at having been taught by an admired teacher. Such an education is of **value** for the whole of one's life."

Rudolf Steiner

"Educate the **will** today, and you set a good **foundation** for the future."

Douglas Gerwin
executive director of the Research Institute
for Waldorf Education, USA

"Students need protection, love and truth, which will help draw forth the essence of their individuality, and, in turn, benefit the world. That is why I teach."

Eric G. Müller
educator and founder of the
Alkion Teacher Training Programme, USA

"See the child, love the child, know yourself: now **teach.**"

Elan Leibner
educator and chair of the
Pedagogical Section Council of North America

Acknowledgements

Many members of the worldwide Steiner-Waldorf community assisted in assembling this book. Our warm thanks are extended to:

Stefanie Allon, Kevin Avison, Neil Boland, Warren Cohen, Robin Cook, Márti Domokos, Loïs Eijgenraam, Ulrike Farnleitner, Douglas Gerwin, Lou Harvey-Zahra, Wolfgang Held, Andrew Hill, Foppe Jellema, Silvia Jensen, Constanza Kaliks, Ronald E. Koetzsch, Richard Landl, Elan Leibner, Carol Liknaitzky, Wolfgang Maschek, Patrice Maynard, Jon McAlice, Eric Müller, Sophia Christine Murphy, Alexander Murrell, Janni Nicol, Irina Ogorodova, Andrew Phethean, Sven Saar, Lucy Schneider, Jill Tina Taplin, Lourdes Tormes, Willem van der Velden, Natalie Will, Femke de Wolff, Megan Young.

Sources

⌢

1. Rudolf Steiner, *The Child's Changing Consciousness*
2. A.C. Harwood, *The Recovery of Man in Childhood*
3. Rudolf Steiner, *Artistic Sensitivity as a Spiritual Approach*, lecture of Feb 2, 1915
4. Francis Edmunds, *Rudolf Steiner Education – The Waldorf Schools*
5. Rudolf Steiner, *The Study of Man*, lecture of Sep 5, 1919
6. Willem van der Velden, written for the teachers at the Zenzeleni school in Khayelitsha, Cape Town, 1999
7. Rudolf Steiner, *Foundations of Human Experience*, lecture of Sep 5, 1919
8. Douglas Gerwin, *Aphorisms on the Roles and Limitations of Technology in Education*
9. Jon McAlice, original quote
10. Rudolf Steiner, *Becoming the Archangel Michael's Companions*, lecture of Oct 15, 1922
11. Eric G. Müller, *Do You Love Your Teachers?: Memoir of a Waldorf Teacher*
12. Janni Nicol, original quote
13. Rudolf Steiner, *How to Know Higher Worlds*
14. Helmut von Kügelgen, 'The Year of the Child', *Love as the Source of Education: The Life Work of Helmut von Kügelgen*
15. Rudolf Steiner, *The Education of the Child*

16. Neil Boland, 'Travels in education: Towards Waldorf 2.0.', *Educational Journal of Living Theories*

17. Rudolf Steiner, *Education for Special Needs*, lecture of July 7, 1924

18. Joan Almon, quoted in Susan Linn, *The Case for Make Believe: Saving Play in a Commercialized World*

19. Rudolf Steiner, *Spiritual Ground of Education,* lecture of Aug 19, 1922

20. Sven Saar, original quote

21. Friedrich Schiller, *On the Aesthetic Education of Man*

22. Federico García Lorca, quoted in Manda J. Nandorfy, *The Poetics of Apocalypse: Federico García Lorca's Poet in New York*

23. Rudolf Steiner, *Becoming the Archangel Michael's Companions*, lecture of Oct 15, 1922

24. Emil Molt, quoted in Sophia Christine Murphy, *Emil Molt and the Beginnings of the Waldorf School Movement*

25. Rudolf Steiner, *Foundations of Human Experience*, lecture of Aug 25, 1919

26. Henning Köhler, *Difficult Children: There Is No Such Thing: An Appeal for the Transformation of Educational Thinking*

27. Daniel Beasley, https://www.steinerwaldorf.org/steiner-education/does-it-work/former-global-scholars/

28. Rudolf Steiner, *The Driving Force of Spiritual Powers in World History*, lecture of March 16, 1923

29. Christy MacKaye Barnes, *For the Love of Literature: A Celebration of Language and Imagination*

30. Rudolf Steiner, *Roots of Education*, lecture of April 17, 1924

31. Henry Barnes, 'Learning that grows with the learner: an introduction to Waldorf education', *Educational Leadership*

32. Rudolf Steiner, *The Child's Changing Consciousness*

33. Johann Wolfgang von Goethe, *Early and Miscellaneous Letters of J. W. Goethe: Including Letters to His Mother*

34. Rudolf Steiner, *Foundations of Human Experience*, lecture of Aug 21, 1919
35. Tilda Swinton, https://www.steinerwaldorf.org/tilda-swinton-speaks-on-steiner-education/
36. Margaret Mead, *Coming of Age in Samoa*
37. Rudolf Steiner, *Education as a Force for Social Change*, lecture of Aug 15, 1919
38. Andrew Hill, original quote
39. Rudolf Steiner, *The Child's Changing Consciousness*
40. Richard Landl, original quote
41. Rudolf Steiner, *How to Know Higher Worlds*
42. Willi Müller, original quote (provided by Eric Müller)
43. Rudolf Steiner, *Education as a Force for Social Change*, lecture of Aug 10, 1919
44. Jens Stoltenberg, https://www.steinerwaldorf.org/steiner-education/does-it-work/former-global-scholars/
45. A.C. Harwood, *The Recovery of Man in Childhood*
46. Jill Tina Taplin, original quote
47. Rudolf Steiner, *Rhythms of Learning*
48. Nelson Mandela, *Long Walk To Freedom: The Autobiography of Nelson Mandela*
49. Rudolf Steiner, *Becoming the Archangel Michael's Companions*, lecture of Oct 15, 1922
50. G.K. Chesterton, *Tremendous Trifles*, revised by Neil Gaiman
51. Rudolf Steiner, *Education as a Force for Social Change*, lecture of Aug 10, 1919
52. Chief Seattle, source unknown
53. Rudolf Steiner, *Renewal of Education*
54. Berta Molt, quoted in Sophia Christine Murphy, *Emil Molt and the Beginnings of the Waldorf School Movement*
55. Rudolf Steiner, *Gesammelte Aufsätze zur Kulturgeschicht 1887–1901*, (GA 31, untranslated)

56. Michael Ende, https://www.steinerwaldorf.org/steiner-education/does-it-work/former-global-scholars/
57. Henning Köhler, *Ruimte voor kinderen*
58. Emil Molt, provided by Sophia Christine Murphy from Emil Molt's diaries
59. Ronald E. Koetzsch, original quote
60. Rudolf Steiner, *Balance in Teaching*, afternoon lecture of Oct 16, 1923
61. Wolfgang Held, in conversation, February 2019
62. A.C. Harwood, *The Recovery of Man in Childhood*
63. Rudolf Steiner, *Education for Special Needs*, lecture of July 7, 1924
64. Warren Cohen, original quote
65. Douglas Gerwin, 'Being Fully Human', *Trailing Clouds of Glory*
66. Rudolf Steiner, *The Education of the Child*
67. Albert Einstein, source unknown
68. Rudolf Steiner, *Education for Adolescents*
69. Wolfgang Maschek, original quote
70. Rudolf Steiner, *Spiritual Ground of Education*, lecture of Aug 19, 1922
71. Patrice Maynard, original quote
72. David Mitchell, *Windows into Waldorf*
73. Julianna Margulies, https://www.steinerwaldorf.org/steiner-education/does-it-work/former-global-scholars/
74. Rudolf Steiner, *Modern Art of Education*, lecture of Aug 17, 1923
75. Yanto Barker, https://www.steinerwaldorf.org/steiner-education/does-it-work/former-uk-scholars/
76. Francis Edmunds, *Rudolf Steiner Education – The Waldorf Schools*
77. Jon McAlice, original quote
78. Rudolf Steiner, *The Education of the Child*
79. Kenneth Chenault, https://www.steinerwaldorf.org/steiner-education/does-it-work/former-global-scholars/
80. Rudolf Steiner, *Kingdom of Childhood*
81. Rudolf Meyer, *Die Weisheit Der Deutschen Volksmarchen*

82.   Rudolf Steiner, *Education for Adolescents*
83.   Jennifer Aniston, https://www.steinerwaldorf.org/steiner-education/
      does-it-work/former-global-scholars/
84.   Rudolf Steiner, *Erziehung zum Leben*, lecture of Feb 24, 1921
      (untranslated)
85.   Johann Wolfgang von Goethe, *The Goethe Treasury: Selected Prose
      and Poetry*
86.   John Davy, *Hope, Evolution and Change*
87.   Rudolf Steiner, *Artistic Sensitivity as a Spiritual Approach*, lecture of
      Feb 2, 1915
88.   Johan Cruyff, https://www.cruyff-foundation.org/en/activities/
      schoolyard14
89.   Emil Molt, provided by Sophia Christine Murphy from Emil Molt's
      diaries
90.   Socrates, source unknown
91.   John F. Gardner, *Education in Search of the Spirit*
92.   Emil Molt, quoted in Sophia Christine Murphy, *The Multifaceted
      Life of Emil Molt*
93.   David Sloan, *Life Lessons: Reaching Teenagers through Literature*
94.   Loïs Eijgenraam, *Leerrijpheid, van Kleuterklas naar groep 3 / klas 1*
95.   Rudolf Steiner, *How to Know Higher Worlds*
96.   Andrew Hill, original quote
97.   Rudolf Steiner, *Introduction to Waldorf Education*
98.   Douglas Gerwin, 'Themes and Dreams of a Waldorf High School',
      Genesis of a Waldorf High School
99.   Eric G. Müller, *Do You Love Your Teachers?: Memoir of a Waldorf Teacher*
100. Elan Liebner, 'Authenticity in Education', *Research Bulletin for
      Waldorf Education*

Floris
Books

For news on all the latest books, and to get
exclusive discounts, join our mailing list at:

florisbooks.co.uk/mail/

And get a FREE book
with every online order!

We will never pass your details to anyone else.

e **will** today, and yo

n for the future. **Enl**

ruth, feel responsib

g **courage** to live. Ir

encouragement eve

the child, know you

e children in **revere**

ve, and send them f

an being is a teache

Educate the **will** too

foundation for the f

stand for **truth**, **feel**

s providing **courage**

much, but **encourag**

child, love the child.

Receive the children

them in **love**, and s

Every human being